ENGLISH/FRENCH



# The Toddler's First 150 animal handbook

by Ashley Lee

ANGLAIS/FRANÇAIS

ENGAGE BOOKS
*Mailing address*
PO BOX 4608
Main Station Terminal
349 West Georgia Street
Vancouver, BC
Canada, V6B 4A1

www.engagebooks.com

*Written by:* Ashley Lee
*Edited by:* A.R. Roumanis
*Translated by:* Franco Leva

FIRST EDITION / FIRST PRINTING



LIBRARY AND ARCHIVES CANADA CATALOGUING IN PUBLICATION

Lee, Ashley, 1995– author
The toddler's first 150 animal handbook :
Text in English and French.
written by Ashley Lee; edited by A.R. Roumanis.

Issued in print and electronic formats.
ISBN 978-1-77437-399-6 (bound)
ISBN 978-1-77437-400-9 (paperback)
ISBN 978-1-77437-401-6 (pdf)
ISBN 978-1-77437-402-3 (epub)
ISBN 978-1-77437-403-0 (kindle)

1. Animaux–Ouvrages pour la jeunesse.
2. Anglais (Langue)–Vocabulaire–
Ouvrages pour la jeunesse.
3. Vocabulaire–Ouvrages pour la jeunesse.
I. Roumanis, A. R., editor
II. Title.

QL49 .L445 2020 J590–DC23
C2020-027725-1F C2020-027728-6F

Nose
Nez
Paw
Patte
Tail
Queue
Feather
Plume
Ears
Oreilles
Fin
Nageoire

Claw
Griffe
Whiskers
Moustaches
Antlers
Ramure
Beak
Bec
Wing
Aile
Mane
Crinière

# Pets

# Animaux Domestiques

Cat

Chat

Ferret

Goldfish

 Furet

Poisson rouge

Guinea pig

Cochon d'inde

Betta fish

Poisson Betta

Hamster

Hamster

Hedgehog

Hérisson

Dog

Chien

Rat

Rat

Mouse

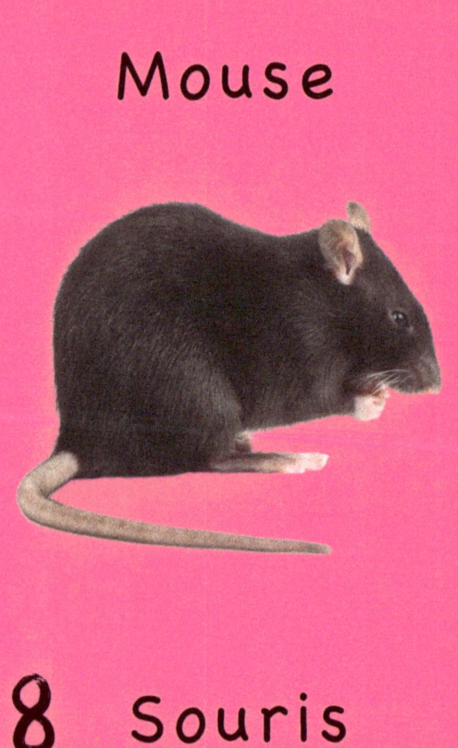

Souris

Budgie

Perruche

# Farm
# Ferme

Pig

Cochon

Horse

Cheval

Pony

Poney

Donkey

Âne

Sheep

Mouton

Emu

Émeu

Yak

Yak

Chicken

Poulet

Rooster

Coq

Turkey

Dinde

Goose

Oie

Goat

Bouc

Llama

Lama

Duck

 Canard

Guinea fowl

Pintade

Alpaca

Alpaga

Ostrich

Autruche

Rabbit

Lapin

Peacock

Paon

# Underground
# Souterrain

Groundhog

Marmotte

Weasel

Belette

Bat

Chauve souri

Mole

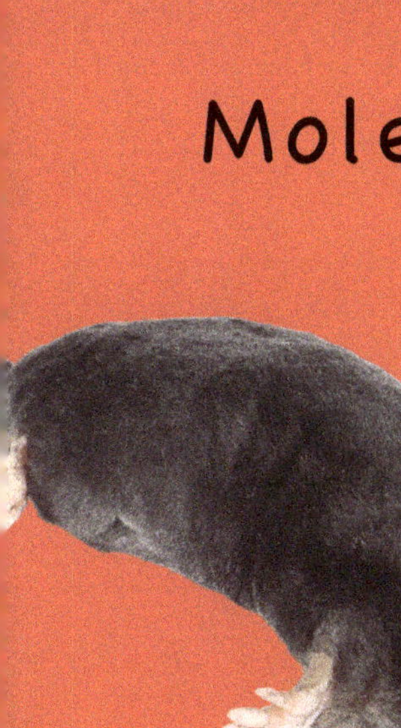

Môle

Worm

Ver de terre

Meerkat

Suricate

Badger

Blaireau

# Forest

# Forêt

Cougar

Puma

Lynx

Lynx

Wolf

Loup

Bear

Ours

Deer

Cerf

Fox

Renard

Snail

Escargot

Toad

Crapaud

Possum

Opossum

Skunk

Moufette

Porcupine

Porc-épic

Racoon

Raton laveur

Chipmunk

Tamia

Squirrel

Écureuil

Beaver

Castor

# Arctic
# Arctique

Muskox

Bœuf musqué

Penguin

Manchot

Reindeer

Renne

Canada goose

Oie canadienne

Polar bear

Ours polaire

Snowy owl

Harfang des neiges

Walrus

Morse

# Aquatic
# Aquatique

Orca

Orque

Salmon

Saumon

Otter

Loutre

Blue tang

Chirurgien bleu

Hermit crab

Bernard l'ermite

Shrimp

Crevette

Lobster

Homard

Clownfish

Poisson clown

Sea lion

Otaire

Shark

Requin

Crab

Crabe

Sea turtle

Tortue de mer

Seahorse

Hippocampe

Sunfish

Poisson lune

Dolphin

Dauphin

Octopus

Poulpe

Squid

Calamar

Jellyfish

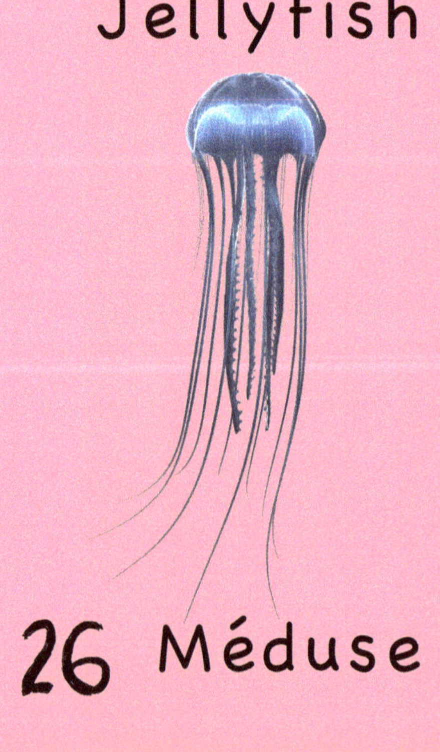

Méduse

Urchin

Oursin

Stingray

Raie

Starfish

Étoile de mer

Marlin

Marlin

Eel

Anguille

# Tropical

# Tropical

Iguana

Iguane

Chameleon

Caméléon

Tiger

Tigre

Tree frog

Rainette

Toucan

Toucan

Parrot

Perroquet

Jaguar

Jaguar

Monkey

Singe

Orangutan

Orang-outar

Gorilla

Gorille

Chimpanzee

Chimpanzé

Flamingo

Flamant

Tarantula

Tarentule

Sloth

Paresseux

Baboon

Babouin

Elephant

Éléphant

Bison

Bison

Aardvark

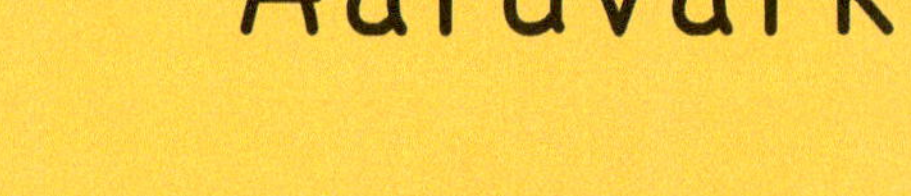

Oryctérope

Hippopotame

Serpent

Gazelle

Gazelle

Scorpion

Scorpion

Koala

 Koala

Panda

Panda

Vulture

Vautour

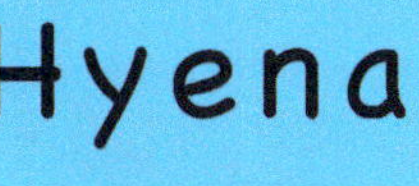

Hyena

Hyène

Camel

Chameau

Lion

Lion

Crocodile

Crocodile

Gecko

Gecko

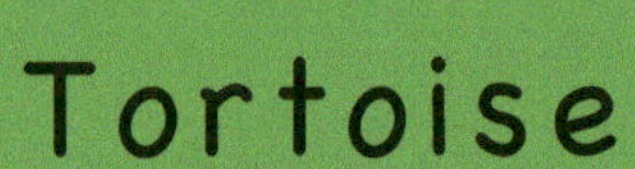

Tortoise

 Tortue

Lizard

Lézard

Giraffe

Girafe

Zebra

Zèbre

Cheetah

Guépard

Boar

Sanglier

# Bugs
# Insectes

Grasshopper

Sauterelle

Ant

Fourmi

Ladybug

Coccinelle

Dragonfly

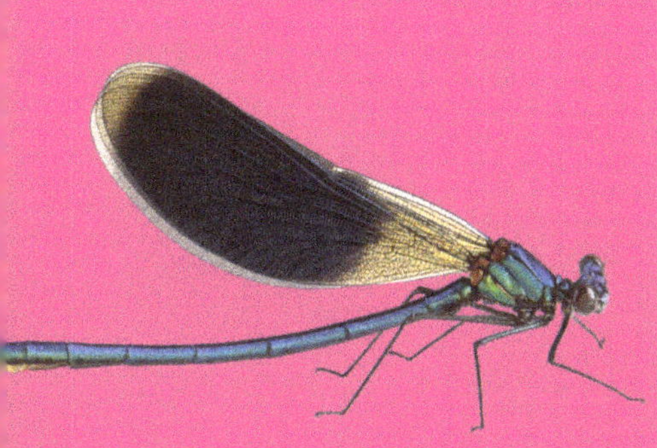

Libellule

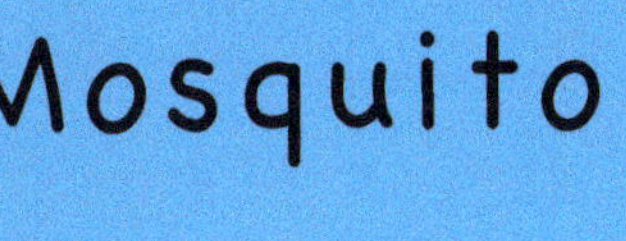

Mosquito

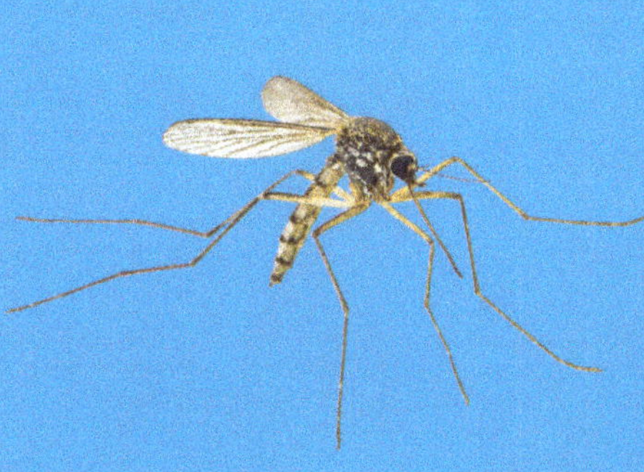

Moustique

raying mantis

Mante religieuse

Cockroach

Cafard

Butterfly

Papillon

Caterpillar

Chenille

Beetle

Scarabée

Wasp

Guêpe

Fly

Mouche

Bumble bee

Bourdon

Moth

Papillon de nuit

Spider

Araignée

# Birds
# Oiseaux

Woodpecker

Pivert

Pigeon

Pigeon

Bluejay

Geai bleu

Robin

Rouge-gorge

Crow

Corbeau

Hummingbird

Colibri

Sparrow

Moineau

Stork

Cigogne

Eagle

Aigle

Pelican

Pélican

Heron

Héron

Seagull

Mouette

Puffin

Macareux

Quail

Caille

Pheasant

Faisan

# activity / activité

Match the following Spanish words to the pictures below.

Faites correspondre ce qui suit aux images ci-dessous.

Can you find:

Pouvez-vous trouver:

**un chat,**
**un singe,**
**une étoile de mer,**
**un écureuil,**
**un canard,**
**un bourdon,**
**un éléphant,**
**un pingouin,**
**et un ver?**

Responder: pingüino

Responder: abejorro

Responder: ardilla

Responder: elefante

Responder: gusano

Responder: pato

Responder: mono

Responder: gato

Responder: estrella de mar

Explore other books at www.engagebooks.com

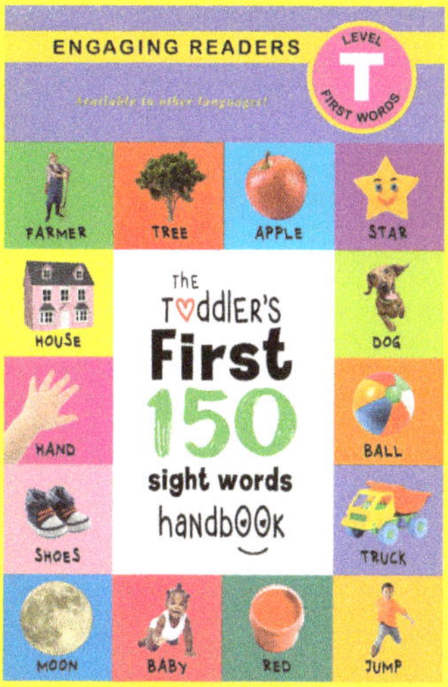


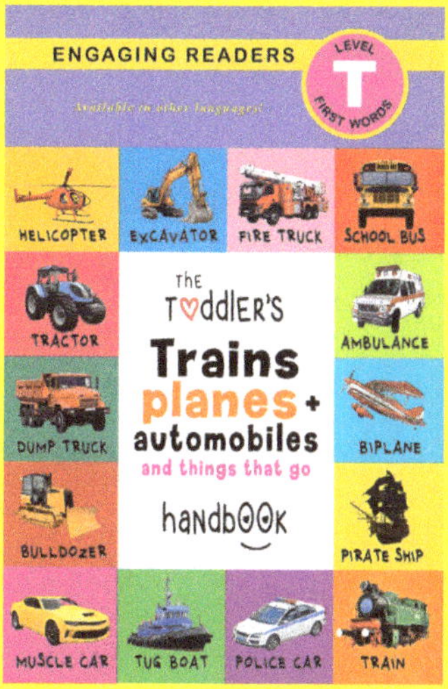


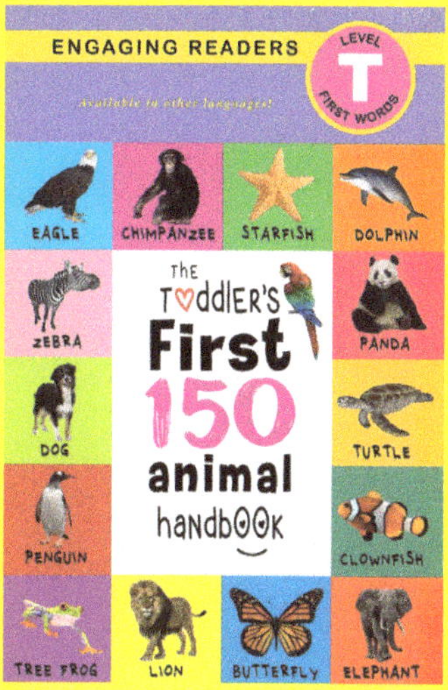


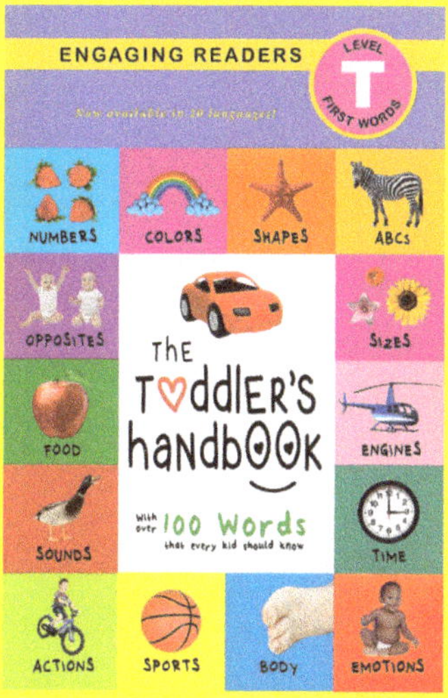


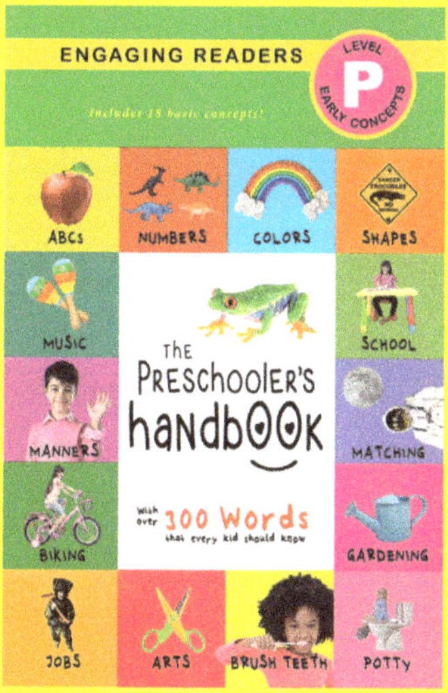


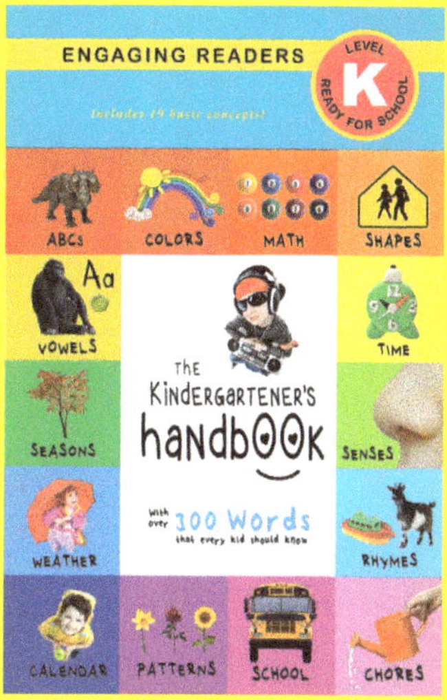


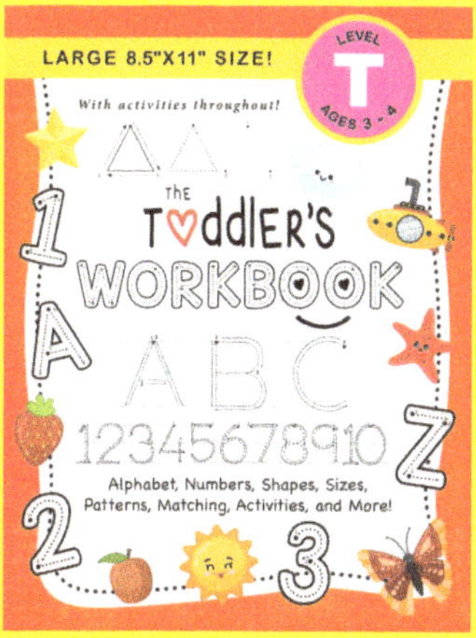


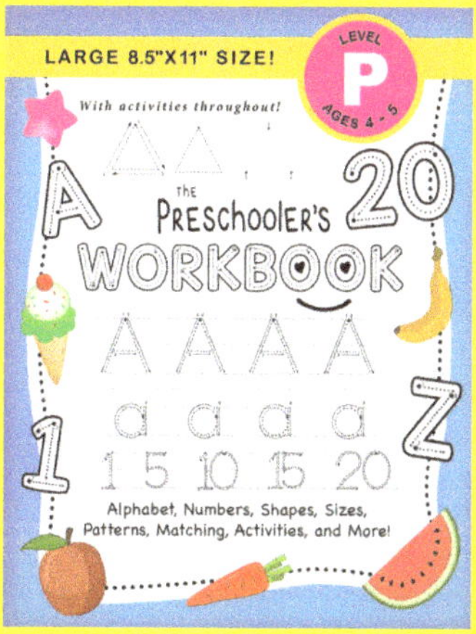


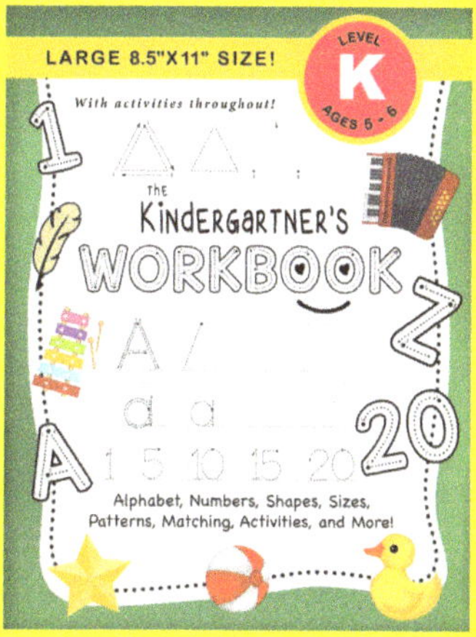


*Have comments or suggestions?*
*Contact us at: alexis@engagebooks.ca*

Show us how you enjoy your **#engagingreaders**. Tweet a picture to @engagebooks for a chance to win free prizes.

www.ingramcontent.com/pod-product-compliance
Lightning Source LLC
LaVergne TN
LVHW051934220826
846093LV00012B/512